Unzipped

Unzipped

a portable guide to the anatomy

of the female customer

by
michele miller

PRESS

Wizard Academy Press
16221 Crystal Hills Drive
Austin, TX 78737
512.295.5700 voice, 512.295.5701 fax
www.WizardAcademyPress.com

ISBN: 978-1-932226-83-6
Library of Congress: 2010938087

Printed in Canada.

*For marketers and business owners everywhere
who give a little piece of their heart
to their customers every day*

Contents

Introduction

A Face in the Crowd

Let's get this over with, shall we?

Women are different from men - very different.

Have you slipped a widget? You can't talk about that. Women have spent the last one hundred years fighting for equality and now you want to talk about how different they are from men? Good god, somebody quick call Gloria Steinem. Just the mention of it might lead people to believe that women are the weaker sex. Don't you realize how dangerous this is, not to mention politically incorrect?

Yes, I do. I'm also pretty sure that's how we got into this pickle in the first place.

We've spent so much time in the last few years waltzing around the delicate balance of gender equality that we've completely forgotten how to embrace the differences between men and women - differences that not only represent who we are as people, but also who we are as *consumers.*

Ultimately, fear of those differences is to blame for the failure of hundreds of well-intentioned marketing strategies and advertising campaigns.

Learning what some of those differences are will be good for you. They are the tools you need to create an effective marketing strategy – a plan and message so powerful, it will transform your business from merely average into one that is positvely extraordinary.

So if you've had a hang-up over gender differences in the past, *get over it.* I hereby give you permission to start selling to women *as* women.

•   •   •

Maybe you still have thoughts in the back of your mind that prevent you from getting started.

"This whole 'Marketing-To-Women' thing is too hard to understand –it's too mysterious, not to mention generic."

You're right, because it should *never, ever* have been about "marketing to women." That's an idea that's too big, too broad, and almost impossible to wrap your brain around.

What it's really about is the **female customer – an individual with specific needs and desires**. We're going to "unzip" a few layers so that we can get you down to a level that allows you to "see her real": As a unique and wonderful individual instead of an aggrandized, impossible-to-understand demographic.

***"I already have a lot of women as customers –
I must be doing something right."***

Maybe. Then again, maybe it's just been sheer, dumb luck.

You sell something that women want and because your competition does a lousy job of marketing, you win by default. Or maybe you're attracting a certain segment of the female demographic but can't seem to get the rest to do business with you. Ever wonder why? There are reasons... and answers that can change all of that for you.

"My product/service isn't feminine enough for her."

While you were focused on the issue of femininity, women...

- Purchased 40 percent of all Hummer H3s and Ford Mustangs in 2007.
- Took control of 56 percent of the consumer electronics market.
- Came close to bringing a major home-improvement retailer to its knees, forcing the company to re-brand itself in order to gain back the female consumer dollars it had lost.

Women don't need "feminine," they need *relevance*, and relevance differs depending on the individual. Keep reading, and you'll discover the two factors that every woman uses to determine relevance.

"If I only focus on women, it will piss men off."
As if the average man ever paid any attention anyway. But I get it. You're afraid of accusations of gender bias, which could mean the loss of what you believe to be your core market. Trust me: If you promise to read and digest the information in this little book, you'll understand how creating the right kind of connection with female customers means you'll also end up with more male customers than you ever dreamed.

"I'll never be able to market to women because I'm not female."

And I'll never be able to run the Kentucky Derby because I'm not Sea Biscuit. Who on earth ever told you that just because a person is a woman, she automatically understands the inner workings of the female customer? When it comes to marketing, it's not about gender, it's about *knowledge.*

•   •   •

Knowledge starts with an understanding of the concept and goals before you. By breaking a large concept down into smaller elements, you'll learn how it works and can use that knowledge to your advantage.

When it comes to doing business with women, the most effective marketing campaigns are built on a foundation of three important pieces of knowledge:

1. **Brain Wiring** A woman's human operating system is your gift from the marketing gods. Every breath she takes, every choice she makes flows on a river of connections. Learning about the differences in the female brain is the first step to truly understanding the potential of a woman to become a fanatically loyal customer.

2. **Inner Perspective** Women are not only different from men; they're different from *each other.* Female customers often have different needs and desires for *the very same product or service.* Going deeper to explore the two elements – energy and time – on which every woman relies for her personal inner perspective will open a door to the **four types of female customers** that are waiting to do business with you.

3. **Language & Communication** A woman's physical wiring doesn't just have control over her decisions; it's responsible for the very words she chooses to use *and* the words to which she responds. Women have

specific language patterns and communication styles that, when revealed, teach you how to create persuasive messages and deliver powerful sales experiences.

This portable guide to the anatomy of the female customer will give you the basic information you need to not only understand her better, but also speak to her in a language that persuades her to hit the BUY button in her brain.

Read it. Spend time thinking about it. Share it with your team, your staff, your boss. Sit it upright next to your computer monitor or tuck it away on the shelf underneath your cash register for easy reference. Most of all *use* it. It will give you the confidence to communicate with women in ways you know are getting through, and will generate new ideas for marketing strategies and campaigns that *work.*

Part One

She's Wired For a Relationship With Your Brand

Chapter One

The View From Here

If I had to guess, I'd say you must be high.

You're working so hard to understand the female customer (and I love you for that). But what are you doing all the way up *there?*

Maybe you've read articles or books or heard marketing experts advise the use of demographic information in order to "capture an aerial view of the marketing-to-women landscape."

That, my friend, is codswallop.

Between you and me, your altitude is much too high (plus the lack of oxygen will make you see pink elephants dancing the Macarena).

The precious, profitable clues that reveal what *re-*

ally makes a customer tick lie hidden *within* every woman walking the planet.

And you don't have to tunnel very far below the surface before hitting the veritable mother lode of clues – the female brain.

• • •

In 1981, Roger Sperry won the Nobel Prize for his research on the "split brain." Sperry was the first modern-day scientist to prove that the left and right hemispheres of the brain have highly specific, designated jobs.

Left Brain Controls:

Language and fluency – the home of nouns
Calculations – mathematics, science
Logic – linear analysis of information

Right Brain Controls:

Spatial relationships
Memories – experiences, emotions, faces
Imagination – visual and auditory

The left hemisphere is the worker bee. It shoulders the grunt work of applying logic to bits of information in order to create an objective reality. How does it do this? By looking for gaps between a linear series of thoughts, then working to plug the holes.

The right brain is the master chef of a giant cerebral kitchen. It supplements left brain thoughts with body language, feelings, and memories to enhance experience and add dimension to life. For the right brain, it's all about **pattern recognition** – seeking out similarities and recognizing

relationships between incoming signals in order to put them together like pieces of a puzzle.

You need your left brain in order to function in every day. But without the playful, imaginative right brain, it would be a pretty dull world. You'd still have the ability to read and speak a phrase like, "pink elephants dancing the Macarena," but you wouldn't be able to *picture* it in your mind's eye. You need your imagination to make it happen.

How can a customer desire your product or service if she cannot first imagine using it? She can't. Ergo, the right brain is your new best friend.

•   •   •

But wait. Everyone has a right brain, not just women. Why should you set your sights on female customers?

Because a woman's brain has <u>four times</u> as many connections between the left and right hemispheres as that of a man's.

That means four times the processing speed.

Four times the horsepower to tap into the right brain of imagination.

Four times the opportunity for you to show her how your business fits neatly into a pattern that already exists inside her mind.

Get it?

She's naturally wired for a relationship with your brand.

Now before you go off all cock-a-hoop and start thinking that all you have to do is "get in touch with a woman's imagination," consider this: **Four times as many connections means she's also four times as likely to send you packing.**

Her special brain wiring attracts a tsunami of incoming signals every minute of the day, so her filtering system has to be mighty strong *and* mighty ornery – a curmudgeonly little troll, standing between you and her TAKE ACTION button.

The words you use in your advertising, and the experience you create in your store, office or on your website, have to be remarkable enough to charm that troll right out of his scratchy little pantaloons. Only then will you gain *and keep* her attention.

Every incoming signal zips down an express lane into her right brain – the home of emotional memory, intuition, and experience.

She's not only reading your advertising or web copy, she's attaching feelings to it. One thoughtfully chosen word can make – or break – you. It can mean the difference between having her flip past the page with your ad on it, or rushing to the Internet in order to find out where your store is located.

When it comes to customer experience, this special brain wiring means that a woman also has a heightened sensitivity to pain. Studies show that she subconsciously compares her current situation with those in her right-brain file drawer of experience. She not only pulls up a memory, she re-enacts the feelings connected with it.

Her emotional memory is so strong, **she doesn't even have to have had the experience herself.** All she has to do is hear a story about a bad experience from a friend or family member, and *her brain registers it as though it was actually feeling pain.* She stores the memory as her own. So, it's up to you whether your message and experience touch the right emotional buttons.

Finally, any neuroscientist will tell you that the **reward behavior** area of the brain (the region that loves dark choco-late, beautiful music, and great sex) is located – where else? – in the right brain.

Sounds like a good place to plant a brand as well, wouldn't you say?

Chapter Two

A Different Kind of Smart

"Do you really think that's a smart move?"

That question was burned into my brain during a mountaintop summer in 1988. I was twenty-seven years old, just getting started in the arts administration business, and had been hired as the director of housing for the Aspen Music Festival. The school had no accommodations of its own and relied on the generosity of local resorts, a strategy that had worked for thirty-eight years. But this particular summer brought with it a staggering pile of housing requests that had been granted without checking the number of available rooms. Needless to say, the balance was not in my favor and it was my job to make sure every student had a place to live.

The week leading up to the festival was a blur of panicked young musicians, contentious city council pow-wows and, ultimately, the opening of a defunct Red Roof Inn to help house all of the students. In meeting after meeting, when I was often the only female in the room, I would present my plans and recommendations to the boss, Bill Vickery. Invariably, at some point during the meeting one person or another would look at Bill and say, "Do you really think that's a smart move?" Bill would stare at my plans, grin, and say, "A different kind of smart, but smart. Let's give it a try." And we did, to great success.

At the time Bill Vickery was my hero, but back then I believed he was just lending support to a young chick with the *cojones* to throw her marbles in with the big boys. Little did Bill or I know that he was actually about twenty years ahead of his time in understanding *female intelligence.*

Traditional science has long claimed that "smart is smart." Men and women are equally intelligent, researchers have said, because of *gray matter* – those amazing little nerve cell bodies that transmit sensory information through the brain.

Equally intelligent? No question about it. But now it turns out that all this time, science only had it half right. It's *where that intelligence comes from* that's one of the biggest surprises of the 21st century.

•   •   •

In 2005, the University of California-Irvine and the University of New Mexico released the results of a major medical study on human intelligence. Gathering a group of forty men and women – with equivalent IQs – researchers using neuroimaging technology to study the intellectual process in the brain. They found that while the capacity for intelligence in each gender may be the same, **the intellectual process that the female brain goes through is very, very different from that of a male.**

On average, **men have more than six times the amount of gray matter** than women do in relation to general intelligence. Men are much better (and faster) at taking individual pieces of sensory information and lining them up to make sense to the brain.

So how do women make up for that imbalance? By possessing nearly **ten times the amount of *white matter.***

And what's the job of white matter? White matter is responsible for **connecting and networking** the cells of gray matter.

A woman's brain relies on white matter to process incoming signals in a way that detects patterns in order to provide a solution.

Bingo!

Reaching out and connecting with a female customer requires a different angle of approach. **She's not really interested in you until you can show how and where you fit into the patterns and connections that are important to her.**

Male   **Female**

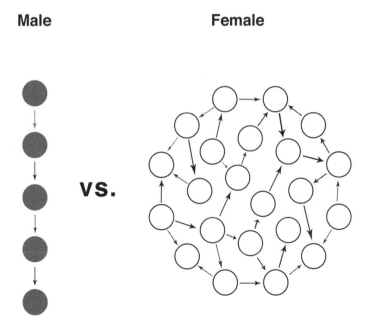

Once you understand that her entire world is built on the concept of connection – not just connection between humans, but also on the *connection* of incoming signals - you'll also realize that you're going to have to start speaking a special language; the *only* language that can make it through the rigorous filtering system in her brain and get her to push the BUY button.

Different kind of smart, indeed. Bill Vickery, you were a genius.

Chapter Three

The Eye of the Female Consumer

Leaning into the open refrigerator, your mother senses you reaching for one of the chocolate chip cookies that are cooling on the kitchen counter and reminds you not to spoil your dinner.

Reading a magazine in the family room, she hones in on the moment you are about to deliver a super-sized nuggie attack on your whiny little brother, and without turning around, issues the Let-Go-Of-Your-Brother-This-Instant-Or-You'll-Hurt-His-Neck-And-Then-You-Can-Tell-Your-Father-About-It-When-He-Gets-Home command.

Wow. What is this amazing power that gives a mommy eyes in the back of her head?

Is it estrogen?

Was she struck by lightning?

Has she fallen victim to an alien invasion of talking walnuts?

No. It's just that vision is literally in the eye of the beholder. Not only are women's brains wired in a unique and wonderful way, *so are their eyes.*

Inside your eye, the retina is the component that allows you to gauge focus, light, and movement. Two important parts of the retina are *cones* and *rods*, which are connected.

The main job of the cones is to allow for focus (especially intense focus on one thing at a time), meaning *greater depth perception.*

The rods of the retina, being extremely sensitive to light, can detect the slightest movement in the visual field, *meaning greater peripheral vision.*

Guess which women have more of: cones or rods? That's right – **rods.**

As a general rule, the female retina has more rods than that of the male, resulting in **greater peripheral vision and the ability to see the "whole picture" all at once.**

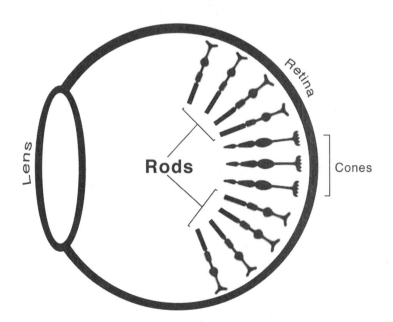

With a brain that's structured for massive signal input and a pair of eyes that possess the peripheral vision of Wonder Woman, the female customer can't help but absorb visual cues that affect how she feels about your business.

These optic bits are automatically catalogued in her brain, directly into a file folder with your name on it. They are the subliminal puzzle pieces that validate her decision about whether or not she wants to be your customer.

What do her eyes register when she encounters your place of business?

To name a few...

- Signage from the road
- Width of parking spaces
- Cracks in the sidewalk
- Landscaping
- Fingerprints on the glass entry door
- Stains on the carpet
- Color of the walls
- Lighting in the store and showcases
- Dusty furniture
- Signage in departments
- Width of the aisles
- Arrangement of product displays
- Proximity of sales staff

Her eyes are working overtime, and all of those incoming signals can be pretty steep competition if you're trying to get her attention. By eliminating as many negative visual cues as you can up front, you will help her mind relax, focus on the task at hand, and be more open to developing an ongoing customer relationship with you.

With eyes like these, female customers form an opinion of you before they ever encounter a member of your staff. What kind of subconscious impression are *you* making?

For an easy and fun way to get a snapshot of how your business rates in the eyball area, download the FREE "Quick Visual Checklist" at www.wonderbranding.com. Have your employees and even some customers go through your store or office with the checklist as well. The results may surprise you, but they'll definitely help you improve your customer experience.

Part Two

The Energy and
Time Equation

Chapter Four

The Business of

Sisterhood

Awhile back, I received a package from my father stuffed with family mementos that date as far back as the late 1800s. Amongst the memorabilia, tucked in between a sepia portrait of my great-grandfather posing with a pack mule at Pike's Peak and a black-and-white candid of my father in 1950s Paris, were photographs of Madeline and Olive.

Madeline was my grandmother and Olive was her older sister. Born around the turn of the 20th century, Madeline and Olive lived near each other for much of their lives, often times

Olive

in the same zip code. As adults, their incomes were similar – sometimes, they had an adequate bank balance; other times, they were as poor as dirt. They each owned their own homes, raised families, and drove large American cars. But never were two sisters more different.

Madeline was quiet and introspective; a chronic illness had left her physically frail. She married young and worked on the family farm, taking waitress jobs when her health would allow. She adored her sons, never missed an episode of *The Ed Sullivan Show,* and enjoyed long car rides in the country most Sunday afternoons after church.

"Moxie" should have been Olive's middle name. A single mother at the age of 16, Olive was hell-bent on providing for herself at a time when job opportunities for women were scarce. She was a secretary, an organist in silent movie theaters, and a registered nurse. She was married several times (that we know of), including one marriage in the 1930s to a Chicago gangster. She swore like a sailor, sipped tea like a princess, and drove like a maniac. Till the day she died at the age of 89, she was, as she liked to put it, "her own woman, damn it."

Madeline

Madeline and Olive were as close as two sisters could

be, but polar opposites in personality. The everyday choices they made, so different from each other's, were based not on where they lived, how much money they made, or which car they drove.

Yet advertisers expected Madeline and Olive to both respond exactly the same way to marketing messages based solely on their "demographics."

They believe that what I call the **Rule of Resemblance** – targeting women by age, income, lifestyle category, or zip code – is their mainsail, when more often than not it's the anchor that prevents them from getting where they need to go.

The Rule of Resemblance strategy usually results in weak response and low (if any) return on investment.

Here's why the Rule of Resemblance fails:

1. **It says that given the same external factors, all women respond equally.** Focusing solely on external circumstances like zip code, income, or age ignores a very important factor in the marketing equation – the internal value system of the individual. The Rule of Resemblance creates an inflated sense of overlap between external characteristics, giving you the false assertion that if a woman lives in targeted zip code, then she also makes a designated income, enjoys a particular lifestyle, and (even more dangerous) lives by a specific code of internal values. Try placing twelve women from the same zip code (even the same city block) in a room and see if their personal values aren't wildly different from each other's. Values, or the chosen ideals a woman lives by everyday, are what brand decisions are based on – not address or income.|

2. **It assumes that every woman has the same time horizon.** As a business owner, your goal is to make money today – but that doesn't mean a woman is ready to buy at the precise moment you're ready to sell. To her, time is more than a date on the calendar; it's also the lens through which she views her outlook on life. That view

may be short-term ("living in the moment"), long-term ("making a difference for the future"), or somewhere in between. Each decision a woman makes is held up to her personal time horizon to see if it fits, and if so, where. Time knows nothing about age, income, or lifestyle demographics, but its function is critical when it comes to determining your importance in her life.

If you've been relying on the Rule of Resemblance, don't be too hard on yourself. You worked hard with the information you were given. And for a long time, it was the biggest and best tool in your kit. But the splintering of the media landscape (500 cable channels?!) and, most importantly, that media explosion called the Internet, have transformed the marketing landscape. The main reason the Rule of Resemblance doesn't work any more is that it doesn't account for the most important part of a woman – *what's inside the customer.*

Attracting women, both as loyal customers and motivated employees, gets more difficult with each passing day. It's up to you to shed the rules of the past and embrace the truth of the future: that **the sisterhood of female customers is based not on a world of similarity, but rather a universe of individuality.**

What will it take? For starters, exploration into the unknown regions of the female values system. Understanding of how her time horizon affects every purchase she makes. And creation of various dialects in the language of marketing that will speak directly to the hearts of different female customers.

No one said this business of sisterhood was easy. But stick with me, and we'll make it more profitable than you can imagine.

Chapter Five

Tapping Her Energy to Build Your Brand

Because a woman has four times the number of connections between the left and right hemispheres of the brain, your female customer's "human operating system" functions more like a web than a railroad track.

Her brain takes in millions of signals and continuously works to reorganize patterns. It then builds networks of those patterns in order to make decisions, strengthen relationships, and devise solutions to everyday challenges.

Connection, both human-based and information-based, affects everything in her life, including her purchasing process.

An enormous amount of energy is required to keep your female customer's operating system performing at an optimum level, day-in and day-out.

Where does that energy come from?

The answer will differ depending on which woman you are talking to. **There is an important, essential difference in how women make their purchasing decisions.**

external   internal

One woman may draw on **external sources of energy** to feel connected. She relies on stimuli from the outside world (such as interacting with groups of people) to charge herself up and get what she needs to make it through the day.

At the other end of the spectrum, you'll find a woman who draws on **internal sources of energy** (like inner thoughts and feelings) for the fuel she needs. She looks inward for guidance, and generates energy through the time she spends thinking and mulling things over.

A group of female customers will all come to the same decision to do business with you, using completely different pathways.

Are you delivering your brand message and product information in ways that compel both types of energies to do business with you?

Here are a couple of examples:

Surfing vs. Dialing

Did you know that one of the biggest reasons you may

be missing out on website revenue is that you don't provide your phone number on the homepage?

There's a large segment of "external energy" customers who, when they are shopping online and have a question, want to pick up the phone and speak to someone. They need the energy charge that comes from connecting with a human being, which cements the sale. There's a reason that websites like Schwan's (www.schwans.com), Office Depot (www.officedepot.com), and Blair Clothing (www.blair.com) keep showing up on the "Top Ten Converting Websites" list - their phone number is not only on the homepage, it's at the top of every page.

Discounting the Ruminator

Too often, in-store sales staff write off the customer who says she's "just looking." It should actually be a clue that she may rely more on internal energy to turn things over in her mind awhile before deciding to make a purchase.

Why are you letting her walk away empty-handed? Wouldn't it be better to have a printed piece on your product or service - one that gives her a little more information, and fills in some of the gaps in her brain when it comes to deciding whether you're the brand for her?

By delivering information to a female customer in the way she needs to see or hear it, you'll be taking an excellent first step toward creating rock-solid brand loyalty.

Remember: She needs premium fuel to charge up enough energy to do business with you. It's up to you to make sure you're putting the right kind of tiger in her tank.

Chapter Six

How Time Influences Her Purchasing Process

Women draw energy from different sources, both internal and external, which means that you need to deliver your message from two different perspectives at all times in order to make sure you're tapping directly into the pipeline of her neurons and planting your brand inside her brain.

But planting a brand is one thing; having the patience to let the seed bloom is another.

Here's where the other critical factor of the female purchasing process kicks in – her **time horizon.**

A woman's **time horizon** is the linchpin of her life; it's the lens through which she looks in order to gauge the effectiveness of the decisions she makes.

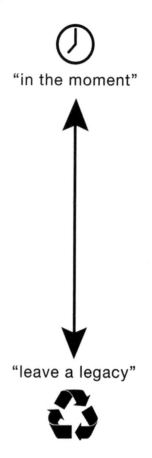

One woman may lean toward living **"in the moment,"** making decisions that to some might seem impulsive, but to her are based on a philosophy that the road of life is short. Her mantra is, *"Carpe diem,* baby!"

Another woman's decision may be influenced by an outlook that this world of ours is bigger than we'll ever comprehend. For her, it's important to plant seeds of love and hope that may never bloom in her lifetime. She wants to **leave a legacy.**

So while our "In the Moment" gal believes that life is an adventure and should be traversed in a red convertible Mustang, our "Leave a Legacy" female desires to make a small dent in the global warming crisis, so she drives a Prius. Neither choice is right or wrong; it's simply a preference that highlights another essential difference in the way female customers make purchasing decisions.

Let's look at a couple of ad examples that make effective use of the "In the Moment" mindset – one, a major brand, the other a local small business.

Skechers – "Shape Ups"

Now you can get in shape without setting foot in a gym! Workout while you walk! New from Skechers... it's Shape-ups, the newest in exercise equipment. Wear your Shape-ups everywhere and anywhere and your body will feel the difference immediately. Skecher Shape-ups are designed to strengthen back, abdomen, buttock and calf muscles, improving your circulation and reducing the impact on your joints and lower back. Today's new walking shoes – finally you can get in shape! Skecher's Shape-ups – your first step toward a healthier you!

Fairview Garden Center – "Not a Gardener"

You know, you don't have to be a gardener to make your backyard beautiful. Hi, this is Brad Rollins from Fairview Garden Center, where we have everything you need to instantly create your own backyard oasis. Colorful hanging baskets in full bloom, beautiful outdoor furniture, decorative trellises... right down to that trickling fountain you've been dreaming of. Why not make this your summer of color, today? Fairview – adding color to your life, inside and out.

Both Skechers and Fairview make good use of words that create imaging of "living life to the fullest, right now." For those female customers that fall into the "In the Moment" time horizon, these ads are compelling and pique a customer's curiosity enough to make her want to check these businesses out.

Now, let's do a one-eighty and look at two ads that focus on the "Leave A Legacy" time horizon.

Lincoln Financial Group – "Hello Future"

Will you spend your retirement in a comfy chair, watching the world go by? Or will you be out there, with your sleeves rolled up, changing the very shape of it? Saying, "Hello, Future." Call your advisor about the powerful resources of Lincoln Financial Group.

Fairview Garden Center – "Trees"

Hi, this is Brad Rollins from Fairview Garden Center. Planning your spring landscaping? Don't forget the importance of trees. Fairview has an unparalleled selection of flowering and shade trees to add texture and beauty to your yard. And fruit trees like apple, pear, peach, persimmon, and pecan, promise to bear tasty memories for years to come. Add curb appeal, backyard beauty, and a family legacy to your yard today, with trees from Fairview! Fairview –adding color to your life, inside and out.

Lincoln Financial Group's ad was part of a series that spoke to many different kinds of women; this copy is from a TV ad that helped create the imagery needed for women to start thinking about planning for retirement. But even if you just read the words, you can immediately see the difference between this ad (telling a story) and the average ad for a financial institution (filled with numbers, plan names and male-based language).

Fairview Garden Center takes the simple idea of trees and builds a story of memories and legacy that any woman focused on the "Leave a Legacy" time horizon would find irresistible.

The important thing to remember is to **never try and speak to both time horizons in one ad.** The copy won't work well, and it will confuse the daylights out of the customer. And the moment you confuse her, you lose her.

Be patient and speak to one time horizon at a time (or, in the case of a website page, have different paragraphs that speak to one time horizon at a time). You will add clarity to her brand decision process, and you'll come out a winner every time.

Part Three

The Four Neighborhoods of Female Consumers

Chapter Seven

Welcome to the

Neighborhood

    I don't know about you, but the thought of a world full of
female consumers scares the livin' bejeezus out of me.

    It's just too big for me to wrap my brain around.

    But a neighborhood of female consumers? That's a lit-
tle less intimidating. It's an easier concept for your noggin
to manage. It makes the whole idea of female purchasing
power seem less like an alien invasion and more like a block
party with really great beer and a kick-ass band.

    Let's say you were moving to New York City. Just the thought
of trying to cope in one of the busiest, largest, most aggres-

sive metropolises in the world could easily overwhelm you.

But it doesn't have to.

Here's the secret to living in New York: **The Neighborhood Concept.**

A New York neighborhood is just a few square blocks in size, each with its own culture and behavior. Focusing on the neighborhood that surrounds you at any given moment helps you to understand and enjoy one microcosm of a much larger society. You get to know the real New York one neighborhood at a time. You begin to appreciate the diverse cultures that are woven together to create a mind-blowing tapestry of humanity. And eventually, you fall in love with a city that initially seemed foreign and out of reach.

What if you applied the Neighborhood Concept to the world of female customers?

What if you could break the consumer world down into manageable microcosms of women, each with a specific culture and pattern of consumer behavior?

You can.

In fact, you already have the knowledge you need to draw the defining boundaries. Neighborhoods of female customers are created through the principles of energy and time horizon.

Energy + Time Horizon = Purchasing Process

Where a female customer gets her energy, combined with her outlook on life, gives you the underlying framework you need in order to build an effective, profitable marketing strategy. It will affect every part of your business, from planning to copywriting to customer service.

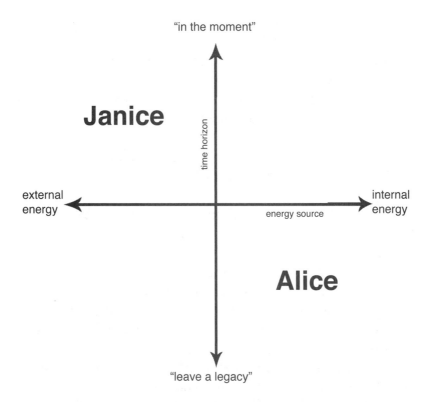

A neighborhood of female customers, each with its own specific culture and behavior, is determined by the point at which energy and time horizon intersect.

Alice lives at the intersection of Internal Energy & Leave a Legacy.

Janice lives at the intersection of External Energy & In the Moment.

Different intersections. Different neighborhoods. Different behavioral patterns.

Different purchasing processes.

Get it?

Learning that women draw upon different energy sources to charge up and get through the day is the first step to understanding that not all women make purchasing decisions in the same way.

Recognizing that women take action based on personal time horizons is the second step.

Overlaying the two factors brings the world of female consumers into focus.

It reveals a small collection of neighborhoods that are based not on age, zip code, or income, but **individual value systems.**

It gives you a longitude and latitude to help you get your bearings. It allows you to not only pinpoint the behavioral locations of your customers, but also uncover a map of the territory so that you know how to get where she is, and where you need to be.

It also makes it easier to predict the questions a customer may have about your business, and help you answer those questions in the language or "dialect" of that neighborhood.

Suddenly, the world of female customers just got a tiny bit smaller.

And more inviting.

And easier to maneuver.

With tremendous profit potential.

How about exploring the neighborhoods of female customers with me? It's guaranteed to be an eye-opener.

And who knows? You just might end up falling in love with a big world that's really not as scary as you first imagined it to be.

Chapter Eight

Unzip Yourself: The Quiz

Pretend that you're moving to a brand new city, one full of promise and exciting prospects for the future.

The moving van is all packed and sits idling at the curb. The driver is aware of the city you're headed for, but still needs to be told the address. It's important for you to know and be able to relay exactly where HOME will be for you; otherwise the driver will just wander aimlessly around the city, burning through fuel, wasting everyone's time and energy.

Let's try something else. Close your eyes. Now, replace all that stuff in the van with your BUSINESS.

Can you tell the driver which neighborhood is HOME for

your business? Or will he drive all over the place, hoping for some customers to flag him down before he runs out of gas?

If you don't know where HOME is, how can you:

- Own a business that has a firm, solid foundation?
- Expect customers to find you?
- Expect employees to understand how the neighborhood functions and strives for growth?

You must know where HOME is for you.

HOME tells your customers what you stand for and how your product, service, and customer experience fit into the puzzle of their daily lives.

HOME helps employees see that even though they might not live in your neighborhood (we do need diversity, after all), they have unique values that they can contribute from their own neighborhoods that will balance yours in a powerful way.

This simple quiz will help you discover which of the Four Neighborhoods of Women you find most comfortable; the place you consider to be HOME in relation to your own energy, time horizon, and personal values.

After you've taken the quiz and rated yourself, you'll have a better idea about you and your business, and how to use your values to attract more customers, make bigger sales, and hire better employees.

SECTION ONE

1. You've created a new section on your website called, "Ask the Owner." Customers send in questions that require specific and interesting answers. What's easier (and least stressful) for you?

    a) Turn on the webcam of your computer to record your answer on video, then upload it to the site
    b) Write out a detailed answer, to be published on the site

2. You've just learned that a customer is perturbed over a mistake made by one of your staff members. How do you prefer to handle the situation?

    a) Call her up to talk about the situation and offer her a discount on future purchases
    b) Send flowers with a handwritten apology

3. Networking within the business community is important. How do you prefer to build your network?

    a) Attend networking events, where you can mingle and meet lots of people
    b) Have lunch or dinner one-on-one with someone who's been referred by a colleague

4. When you are shopping for a big-ticket item, which do you prefer?

    a) Ask for opinions/referrals from friends and colleagues
    b) Conduct extensive online research

5. Which news anchor best reflects your business style?

    a) Katie Couric
    b) Diane Sawyer

6. You're shopping in a bookstore. Which shelf are you most attracted to?

    a) Staff Picks
    b) Critic's Choice

7. When you go shopping, you:

    a) Like to browse
    b) Buy exactly what you need and leave

8. When you conduct a meeting, what is its structure?

    a) General get-together, topics discussed on the fly, brainstorming
    b) Fixed agenda in a strict time frame

9. You're attending a marketing seminar. What kind of exercises do you prefer?

    a) Working with a group to brainstorm and generate ideas
    b) Working on your own to mull over possibilities

10. Your 50th birthday is approaching. You ask your spouse to give you:

    a) A long weekend in Vegas with three of your best friends
    b) A week at a writer's retreat where you can work on your novel

SECTION TWO

1. What best describes your business' marketing strategy?

   a) Keeping an ear to the ground for new ideas to try ahead of the competition
   b) Picking a specific marketing idea and following it through to its conclusion

2. When it comes to your company, which kind of changes do you feel more comfortable with?

   a) Fast, active, and quick to change
   b) Slow, focused, and planned out

3. Which statement best describes your philosophy about business?

   a) I'm just doing this till something more exciting comes along
   b) I'm building this company to hand down to my children

4. You have just learned that there's a problem with one of your staff. What do you do?

   a) Talk to your managers to gain insight, then wait to see if it happens again
   b) Take the employee aside the moment you hear of the problem, to address it head-on

5. You've just been assigned as a team member for a new project. Who would you rather have as your project leader?

   a) Martha Stewart
   b) Hillary Clinton

6. When you attend a meeting, are you more focused on:

   a) The ideas that everyone in the room is generating
   b) Wondering if the meeting will end on time

7. Which way do you prefer to work?

   a) Being open to opportunity; maintaining as much flexibility as possible
   b) Sticking to a calendar and a plan of attack

8. Which is harder to tolerate in your staff:

   a) Uncooperativeness
   b) Incompetence

9. When conducting marketing research for your business, which do you prefer?

   a) Talking directly to customers, vendors, and staff
   b) Surveys & focus groups created by an outside research consultancy

10. It's holiday time. What gift do you give to your employees?

    a) Gift certificate to a 5-star restaurant
    b) Gift certificate for donation to the charity of their choice

Using the chart on the next page, check off either "a" or "b", depending on how you answered each question. Tally the number in each column for Part One and circle the letter at the bottom (E or I) for which you had the most checkmarks. Repeat for Part Two.

•   •   •

Make note of your letter combination from Parts One and Two (EM, EL, IM, or IL) and read on to discover exactly what this means for you and the success of your future marketing strategy.

E= External Energy
I= Internal Energy
M= In the Moment
L= Leave a Legacy

Answer Key

Section One

	a	b
1)	☐	☐
2)	☐	☐
3)	☐	☐
4)	☐	☐
5)	☐	☐
6)	☐	☐
7)	☐	☐
8)	☐	☐
9)	☐	☐
10)	☐	☐
	E	I

Section Two

	a	b
1)	☐	☐
2)	☐	☐
3)	☐	☐
4)	☐	☐
5)	☐	☐
6)	☐	☐
7)	☐	☐
8)	☐	☐
9)	☐	☐
10)	☐	☐
	M	L

Chapter Nine

Your Quiz Results:

What It's All About, Alfie

Bravo to you for taking the Unzipped Quiz.

You now have a better idea of the kind of energy you need, as an individual, to charge yourself up and get through the day. Maybe this information comes as a revelation; if you're an E, you probably now know why you're so drained after sitting in a cubicle all day by yourself, staring at a computer. If you're an I, it may comes as a relief to better understand why you avoid those networking events with big rooms full of strangers.

You also have a better sense of your time horizon. Do you

own or work for a business that others seem to love, but you find boring? Do you have a job reading financial reports all morning long, anxious for lunchtime when you can surf the web for exotic travel deals? Are you working in a fashion boutique but secretly yearn to start a non-profit organization or work for a company that's making a difference in education, health, or the environment? Knowing your time horizon makes all the difference in setting out goals and strategies for both your personal and professional lives.

As a business owner, the answer of which neighborhood you belong should immediately tell you three things:

1. **Why you are attracting a certain segment of the female consumer market.** Most likely, you are very comfortable in your neighborhood. You exhibit the strongest characteristics of that neighborhood and you know how to speak the language. Because of that, you're naturally attracting the segment of female customers that share your values and language. In other words, *people who are just like you.*

2. **How to strengthen your existing marketing.** Because you're so familiar with the territory, it should be easy for you to think of ways and make plans to strengthen your strategy, messaging, and customer experience for this specific segment of female consumers.

3. **How to balance your staff according to neighborhood.** Have you been hiring staff that is too much like you? It's an easy trap to fall into. You feel that you have "shared values" with an employee, which is good. But when the scales tip too far in the direction of what you're most comfortable with, *you're not going to be able to serve the other neighborhoods of women like you should.*

What would be *more* effective is to have candidates take the Unzipped Quiz when you're interviewing them, in order to get a good balance of values and strengthen your business from within. It's also good to have current employees take the quiz to give you a better sense of what they stand for as individuals, and to ensure that you have placed them in a job in which they can excel and grow.

The answer of which neighborhood you fit into should also tell you this: You still have a lot of work to do if you want to grow your business.

You need to explore and discover what makes the other neighborhoods of women tick. You need to reach out in a language that speaks directly to the heart of each customer. Only then will you start attracting a new and diverse customer base.

It's not the easiest work in the world, but it doesn't have to be the most difficult, either.

Let's look at each of the Four Neighborhoods of Women in a little more detail, to give you a head start toward understanding what's important to each, both in terms of advertising and customer experience. Making a few subtle changes to accommodate each could be just the thing you and your staff need to elevate your business to the next level.

Chapter Ten

Neighborhood #1:
The Regal Queen (EM)

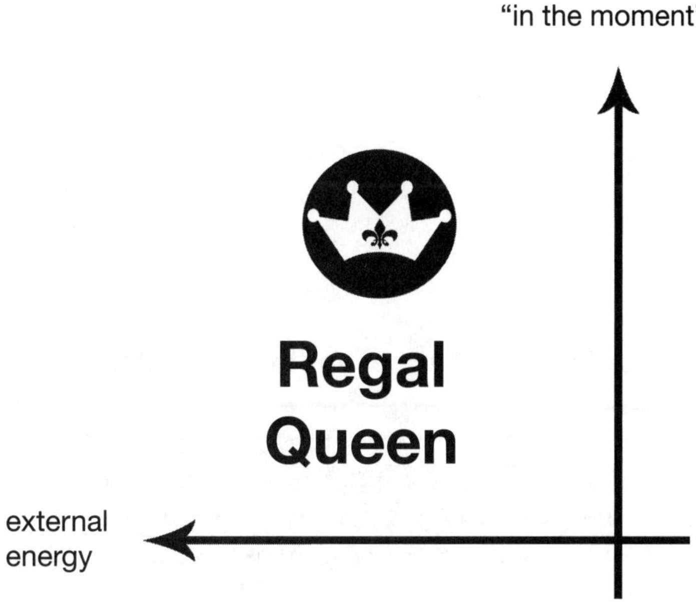

"in the moment"

**Regal
Queen**

external
energy

Energy: External
Time Horizon: In the Moment

Relying on outside forces for energy, and with a "seize the day" mentality, the Regal Queen is the most spontaneous of the four customer types.

She is on the lookout for trends and new things to try when they catch her mind's eye.

She is the most flamboyant and outgoing of the four types, and likes to think of herself as being "unconventional."

She's going to be the customer who loves last-minute bargains, as well as in-store displays at the front of the store featuring "new and cool" items that have just arrived.

Her greatest fear? Being bored.

•   •   •

How would you write copy for the Regal Queen?

Downy "Simple Pleasures" Fabric Softener
Every woman has many sides. Express each one more with Downy Simple Pleasures. Feel more calm with new Downy Lavender Serenity... Feel more daring with Spice Blossom Dare... Feel more elegant with Orchid Allure. Now all have new "in-scent pearls" that help you express every side of you. Downy Simple Pleasures.... Feel more.

McMinn's Furniture

Tired of that boring old room? Hey, you're not dull. Your living space shouldn't be either! Hi, this is Tom McMinn from McMinn's Furniture, where you can give your room an "instant makeover" today. Drop by to see one of our "room stylists" at McMinn's Furniture, 3323 Andrews Highway in Odessa. We'll help you rearrange your current furniture, add a piece, or even totally redo. And we've got what you'll need in stock, so your new room can be a reality in no time at all. It's your space. Make it live the way you want it to!

On-The-Go-Gourmet

On-The-Go Gourmet is the exciting new way to try unique, delicious dishes from around the world. Choose your recipe beforehand, or pick one to try on a whim when you arrive. On-The-Go Gourmet always has everything you need for every dish in our recipe book. Stop losing sleep over what to feed the family – spend your time creating instead!

In one short paragraph, you capture her interest through imaging and language that not only feels familiar to the Regal Queen, it also piques her curiosity. It should sound inviting and, depending on your product or service, even a bit exotic. It's persuasive language that speaks directly to the heart of the Regal Queen and encourages her to give it a try.

The Regal Queen has a turbo purchasing process, which means she can be intrigued by what you offer, but is also easily distracted. If you're writing a page of website copy, make sure your first paragraph speaks to the Regal Queen. With in-store displays, place them near the front of the store or at the checkout counter.

If your copy and customer experience deliver what you

promise, the Regal Queen will not only return again and again, she'll tell all her friends about you and become your biggest word-of-mouth champion.

Chapter Eleven

Neighborhood #2
The Warrior Princess (IM)

"in the moment"

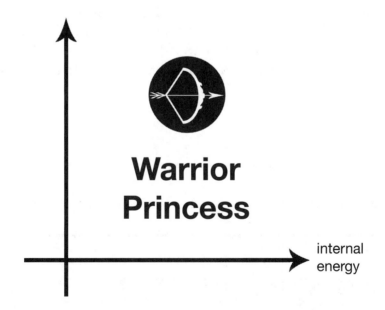

Warrior Princess

internal energy

Energy: Internal
Time Horizon: In the Moment

Moseying on over a few blocks to a new neighborhood, we find the Warrior Princess. What's she all about and how does it affect her buying process?

Like her sister, the Regal Queen, the Warrior Princess lives "in the moment," which means she is quicker to react to incoming signals. But she gets her energy internally, preferring to rely on her inner self for contemplation and decision-making. A bit of a contradiction, but hey – that's life.

To say that the Warrior Princess is competitive is an understatement. Even her leisure activities often involve some kind of self-improvement or competition (even if it's only with herself).

The Warrior Princess is looking for the absolute best; "cutting edge," "certified," and "state-of-the-art" are phrases that get her buying mojo going. But take care in using phrases like that – **you need to be able to deliver on your promise.**

Her big question will be, "So you're all that? PROVE IT." If you can't, she'll leave you in the dust (and then tell her friends about how much you suck like a Hoover).

But deliver superiority on a consistent basis, and she'll be your biggest champion.

Her biggest fear? Missing out on something that is world-class.

•   •   •

How would you write copy for the Warrior Princess?

Kate Walsh – Cadillac CTS ad

In today's luxury game, the question isn't whether or not your car has available features like a 40-gig hard drive. It isn't about sun-roofs or sapelli wood accents, pop-up nav screens, or any of that. No, the real question is: when you turn your car on... does it return the favor?

Fairview Garden Center

Don't you just love to drive your neighbors crazy? Hi, this is Brad Rollins from Fairview Garden Center. You may not be an avid gardener but you still love a beautiful backyard. Fairview has a riot of colorful blooms, containers and decorative add-ons that will instantly transform your yard into an oasis.. and have your neighbors asking, "How did you do that?" Create your next backyard masterpiece with Fairview – we make it easy! Visit us on Holly Springs Road between 1010 and Penny Road in Raleigh.   Fairview... adding color to your life, inside and out.

On-The-Go-Gourmet

The award-winning staff of On-The-Go Gourmet has a combined 40 years of food experience with some of the finest restaurants in the region. As certified master chefs and teachers, your "gourmet sherpas" will guide you through an efficient, state-of-the-art cooking process that creates gastronomical masterpieces in record time. It's not just cooking – it's a gourmet meal that will have your family and friends giving you a standing ovation!

The Warrior Princess wants to believe that she's getting not only the best, but also the hippest (with an "In the Moment" time horizon, that makes her similar to the Regal Queen). She's a cool customer, and above all, wants respect from sales staff – respect that acknowledges her own savvy. Show her you can walk the talk, and she'll keep coming back to you for more.

Chapter Twelve

Neighborhood #3:
The Healer (EL)

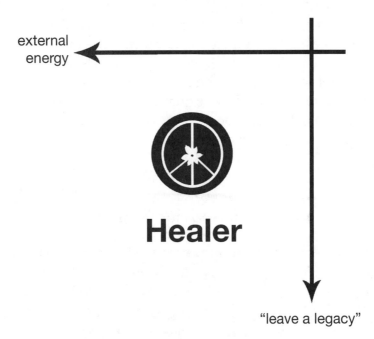

external
energy

Healer

"leave a legacy"

Energy: External
Time Horizon: Leave a Legacy

Let's head south on our time horizon to a neighborhood that's more interested in planting a community garden than partying till 3 a.m.

Welcome to the neighborhood of the Healer.

What's she all about and how does it affect her buying process?

The Healer's time horizon is based more on "leaving a legacy." For her, making decisions that have an immediate impact on her life are not as important as planting seeds that may never bloom in her lifetime – often for the betterment of future generations.

She's usually considered to be the "caregiver" of loved ones, friends, and working units. She is the most humanistic of the neighborhoods and tends to think of her circle as extended family.

She gets charged up from being around others, just like the Regal Queen, but the difference is that because of her long-term time horizon, her purchasing process will be slower.

Her desire for "connecting" with others leads the Healer to be on the lookout for experts to guide and teach her.

Of all the neighborhood types, the Healer is the strongest candidate for a customer experience that doesn't just satisfy, it makes her actually feel good. Feelings are a strong driver in influencing her decisions.

•   •   •

How would you write copy for the Healer?

Giant Foods "Natures' Promise"

At Giant, we realize that "natural and organic" isn't just a way to shop, it's a way of life. That's why we offer "Nature's Promise," a convenient solution to promote your family's health, naturally. Nature's Promise – just another way Giant brings you the best of the best, each and every day.

McMinn's Furniture

*Dreaming of a home where family and friends love to be...
sharing the warmth of a cozy fire and the comfort of a simple
family meal? Hi, this is Tom McMinn for McMinn's Furniture,
your family owned and operated furniture store. At McMinn's,
your dreams can become a reality. We've been helping family
folk just like you create happy homes for more than 37 years.
Why not let us help with yours? Let's get together soon, at Mc-
Minn's Furniture, 3323 Andrews Highway in Odessa.*

On-The-Go-Gourmet

*Even if you're new to the kitchen, On-The-Go Gourmet makes it
easy to be a "dinner superhero" to your family. We have all the
ingredients and equipment you need, and our cooking experts
are on hand to help every step of the way. You'll love working
with our "gourmet sherpas" in preparing meals; we're there as
much as you need us (be sure to ask about our private tutoring
sessions). Success – and a great deal of fun – is guaranteed!*

Right out of the gate, the copy speaks to the Healer because it's not about her, but her family. Phrases like, "promote your family's health, naturally," and, "let's get together soon" speak directly to the heart of the Healer.

Keep your eye out for the Healers that walk through your door. You'll recognize them by their willingness to start a conversation, and the questions they lob at you in order to learn about your product or service. In-store displays that feature "Staff Picks" are popular with Healers, because it's like getting a recommendation from a friend or family member.

Listen carefully, make a connection, and be patient. Show her the way, and she'll be your customer for life.

Chapter Thirteen

Neighborhood #4:
The Guardian (IL)

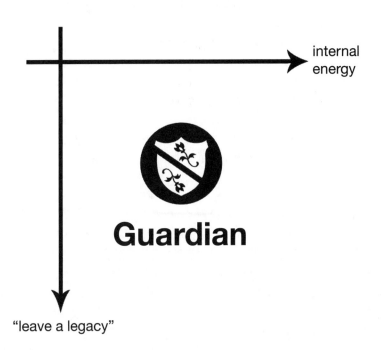

internal
energy

Guardian

"leave a legacy"

Energy: Internal
Time Horizon: Leave a Legacy

Like the Healer, the Guardian's title is self-explanatory. Considering that she gets much of her energy internally and views life on the "Leave a Legacy" time horizon, it should come as no surprise that she is most often the gatekeeper for family, friends, and work colleagues.

The Guardian tends to be more introspective, taking her time in the buying process. Not understanding this could drive a business owner to the edge of batty – it sometimes feels like she'll never make up her mind.

She may seem aloof to you. Don't make the mistake of thinking of her as a "cold fish." There's a lot going on under the surface, and what you may perceive as uncaring is exactly the opposite.

Always remember: the Guardian does not run on feelings like the Healer. In fact, the Guardian is often baffled by people who rely on emotion as part of the process. She prefers to deal with details and facts.

If a woman walks through your door with a copy of Consumer Reports under her arm, it's likely she's in Guardian mode; she's done a great deal of research and is just looking for a few more facts or details to tip her over into your "win" list.

Being the expert with patience will not only get her business, it will cement her loyalty for the long haul.

●   ●   ●

How would you write copy for the Guardian?

Hyundai – "Assurance"

Whenever you buy a new car, you have to sign a contract. But what about the company selling it to you? Where's their signature? Introducing "Hyundai Assurance," Now, finance or lease any new Hyundai and if you lose your income in the next year, you can return it with no impact on your credit. Sound too good to be true? Come and see us, and we'll put it in writing for you. Visit hyundaiusa.com for details.

New Balance San Antonio

Sometimes, life just isn't fair. Why should working so hard to get healthy hurt so much? Well, it shouldn't! Hi, this is Rob Kaufman from New Balance San Antonio. Walking, jogging, running – even the simplest fitness regimens can cause pain. Why? Because you're probably wearing a shoe that wasn't made for your foot. You may be suffering from overpronation, which is just a fancy way of saying that each time you take a step, your foot rolls in more than it should. That forces your big toe to handle most of the work needed to push off the ground for your next step. And THAT means your shins, ankles, and knees are vulnerable to injury. Let New Balance San Antonio make the hurt go away, with a pair of motion control or stability fitness shoes. Crafted according to 88 points of designated fit, and with more than 40 models to choose from, you'll find the shoe that will make getting healthy feel great! Roll in to New Balance San Antonio today and make your hurt go away.

On-The-Go-Gourmet

For the cost of two nights' worth of pizza, On-The-Go Gourmet gives a family of four dinner for a week. With a wide variety of recipes, there's something for everyone. And there's no hassle – we supply everything you need, from ingredients to mixing bowls to mop up. You choose your recipe beforehand and we'll have everything waiting for you upon your arrival. Just mix, cook and go!"

Details and efficiency are what ring the Guardian's bell. In this copy, she immediately resonates with phrases like "expertise and knowledge," and her mind is put at ease about the efficiency of the process itself. It's appealing for not only its value, but also for its to-the-point message: Quality and style, backed by a rock-solid promise.

Make sure every member of your sales staff is highly trained in the details and knowledge about your product or service. Above all, create a highly efficient customer experience that "gets her in and out" without any hassle. Deliver that on a consistent basis, and the Guardian will feel safe and secure doing business with you.

Chapter Fourteen

Extreme Makeover:

Retail Edition

How far would you go to really deliver remarkable customer service? Welcome to Retail Gladiators – your challenger is Sleep Squad.

Sleep Squad is a mattress retailer based in greater Chicago that uses every weapon in its arsenal when it comes to capturing the hearts of customers. Founder and CEO Michael Cote has a keen sense for business opportunity. As he said in a recent interview, "It wasn't like I woke up one morning and decided I wanted to be the mattress king. I wanted to find the worst experience and turn it into something people could brag about to their friends. After we did that, we tried to figure out everything about shopping for mattresses that people really despised."

Cote did his homework. Then, he turned the mattress world on its head.

Sleep Squad has no need for brick-and-mortar retail stores. Why stay in one place when the company can come to *you*? Sleep Squad has reinvented the mattress business with a fleet of portable showrooms that pull up to a home (or even an office!) and offer customers a customized mattress-buying experience.

The Sleep Squad website is breathtaking in its simplicity. It gives you all the information you need on how to test and buy a mattress in four easy steps. You can order online (Internal Energy) or pick up the phone and talk to a specialist (External Energy).

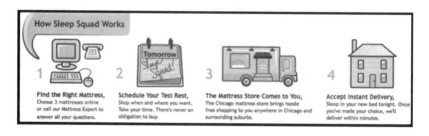

Need a mattress by noon? They've got you covered (In the Moment).

 They not only remove your old mattress, they recycle it (Leave a Legacy).

 The portable showrooms are decorated like bedrooms, with mattresses you can try and choose on the spot (Regal Queen).

 Sleep Squad carries over 150 models of the finest mattresses, compared to an average of 45 in ordinary stores (Warrior Princess).

 They bring your choice of mattress to you, along with three or four alternatives just in case you'd like to do more comparison (Guardian).

 Climate control is an absolute must for ultimate comfort; the showroom's system regulates heat in the winter and air conditioning in the summer.

 The representative gives you some basic information on each mattress, then steps outside and waits so that you can try the mattresses for as long as you like (Healer).

 If it's snowing like crazy and a woman wants to walk from her house to the showroom in her fuzzy slippers? No problem. The staff shovels a path right up to her door.

From inventory, to jacking the trailer for safety, to handling customer introductions, Sleep Squad has it nailed with a comprehensive staff training and maintenance system. But there's one more thing that makes Sleep Squad the success it is:

Members of the sales staff do not work on commission, but instead receive bonuses based on customer satisfaction, whether the customer made a purchase or not.

The pressure to "make the sale" is off. The ultimate goal is to give the customer a remarkable experience – one that she'll tell her friends, family, and colleagues about. In the end, everyone wins – the company, which usually gets the sale; the sales person, who gets a bonus, and the customer, who can finally get a good night's rest.

Sleep Squad does what I've been trying to show you in this step-by-step guide – they've developed a marketing strategy and system that resonates with the internal values of all Four Neighborhoods of Women. This is the kind of business you should seek out, study, and then apply the principles to your own business. It may require an extreme make-over, but if you don't start now, when *will* you start?

Chapter Fifteen

Totally Unzipped:
The Final Secrets

In this portable guide to the anatomy of the female customer, you've learned two things:

1. **Women are wired to fall in love with your brand.** The female brain has four times the number of connections between the left and right hemispheres, which means she has a super-powered purchasing process and great depth in the areas of imagination and emotion. But that information doesn't automatically make her your customer. You're going to have to put some heave-

ho into the work you need to do in order to plant your brand in the reward behavior area of her right brain.

2. **Women are not only different from men, they are different from each other.** Slap pink on your packaging and base your marketing strategy on demographics, and you'll fall flat on your face. Create a strategy that acknowledges the differences in women's energy and time horizons, and you'll capture her heart every time.

If you ascribe to the theory of the Four Neighborhoods of Women and can generate a marketing strategy and campaign that resonates with the internal value systems of all four Neighborhoods, you can't help but succeed in a big way.

If you've read this far, I have a couple of final secrets for you – the "secret sauce" that will help you put the final pieces of the puzzle in place as to why this methodology will work so well for you:

Women are transient – they move around to different Neighborhoods. Very few people live in the same neighborhood all their lives, and it's the rare woman who processes information based on the same energy/time horizon quadrant all her life. Depending on internal and external circumstances:

   a. Most women overlap the characteristics of two neighborhoods at a time – you probably noticed this yourself when you looked at the results of your own quiz.

   b. A woman's outlook changes as she passes through various life stages, which means she could very well live in all four Neighborhoods at different points in her life.

The message for you is, **don't worry about neglecting potential customers**. If you find that you excel in delivering a knockout product and customer service to a particular neighborhood or two, go with it. The odds are that she's eventually going to be living in one of your neighborhoods. Don't let me stop you from working toward giving all four Neighborhoods your best, but do it gradually. Focus on one neighborhood till you *own it,* then move on to the next.

3. **Men function on the energy/time horizon quadrant as well.** They, too, have a right brain that processes an emotional connection to a brand. But the smart thing to always do will be to focus on women first because of their purchasing power, their brain power, and connection power. Don't worry – do it right and you'll have men lining up to do business with you as well.

Use this guide as the handy-dandy reference it was meant to be. Take the quiz. Think about the internal values and needs of different female consumers. Create an exceptional customer experience for one neighborhood, then move on to the next. And always remember the importance of balancing your staff according to Neighborhoods. They're going to fill the gaps that you can't see, and make the connections that will give you a big picture of big profit.

Go forth, and unzip your business. I think you'll be amazed at what you will achieve.

 **Michele Miller** is a partner in the Wizard of Ads marketing firm, working with businesses of all sizes across North American, including Best Buy and Timberland. She maintains a busy schedule as an international speaker on the topics of advertising and marketing to women.

Michele is the author (with Holly Buchanan) of *The Soccer Mom Myth*, which was featured on Amazon.com's "Top Twenty Bestsellers" in the marketing category. She has written a marketing column for Inc.com; her blog, WonderBranding, has won many awards and is included on the prestigious "Best of the Web" list compiled by *Forbes*.

•   •   •

To learn more about Michele, speaking engagements, workshops, and consulting opportunities, visit www.wonderbranding.com.